Mastering the Art of Market Research : Uncovering Insights for Business Growth

Frederic BEHE

Chapter 1: Introduction to Market Research

Chapter 1 provides an overview of market research and its importance in today's business world. Market research is a crucial tool for businesses of all sizes as it helps them understand the needs and preferences of their customers, stay ahead of industry trends, and make informed business decisions.

This chapter begins by defining market research and exploring the various types of research methods that businesses can use to gather data. It also highlights some common mistakes to avoid when conducting market research and emphasizes the importance of defining the scope of research before starting any project.

By the end of this chapter, readers will have a good understanding of the role of market research in business, the different types of research methods available, and the importance of careful planning and preparation before conducting any research. This knowledge will form the foundation for the rest of the book, which will delve into the various stages of market research in more detail.

1.1 Understanding the importance of market research

Understanding the importance of market research is a fundamental aspect of the book, and it is critical to discuss its significance in more detail in section 1.1 of Chapter 1.

Market research helps businesses make informed decisions by providing them with valuable information about their target market, industry trends, competitors, and other relevant factors. By conducting market research, businesses can identify new opportunities, improve their products and services, optimize their marketing strategies, and stay ahead of the competition.

Market research can also help businesses save time and money. By conducting research before making significant investments, businesses can reduce the risk of failure and avoid costly mistakes. They can also use market research to optimize their spending and allocate their resources more effectively.

Market research helps businesses build stronger relationships with their customers. By understanding their customers' needs and preferences, businesses can tailor their products and services to better meet their customers' expectations. This can lead to increased customer satisfaction, loyalty, and advocacy.

Market research is crucial in today's fast-paced and ever-changing business environment. Markets are constantly evolving, and businesses need to stay up-to-date on the latest trends and developments to remain competitive. Market research provides businesses with the insights they need to adapt to these changes and stay ahead of the curve.

Understanding the importance of market research is essential for any business looking to succeed in today's marketplace. By conducting effective market research, businesses can make better decisions, optimize their resources, and build stronger relationships with their customers.

1.2 Types of market research

There are two main types of market research: primary research and secondary research.

Primary research involves collecting new data directly from the target market. There are several methods of primary research, including:

- Surveys: Surveys involve asking people a series of questions about their opinions, behaviors, and preferences. Surveys can be conducted online, by phone, or in person.

- Interviews: Interviews involve speaking directly with individuals to gather more in-depth information about their experiences, motivations, and preferences. Interviews can be conducted one-on-one or in groups.

- Focus Groups: Focus groups involve bringing together a small group of people to discuss a specific topic in detail. The group is typically led by a moderator who asks questions and facilitates the discussion.

- Observation: Observation involves watching people in their natural environment to gather data about their behaviors and preferences.

Secondary research, on the other hand, involves gathering data that has already been collected by other sources.

There are several sources of secondary research, including:

- Government data: Governments collect and publish data on a wide range of topics, including demographics, economic trends, and industry statistics.

- Academic research: Researchers conduct studies and publish papers on various topics that can be useful for businesses.

- Industry reports: Industry reports provide information on specific markets or industries, including market size, trends, and competitive analysis.

- Company reports: Companies publish annual reports that provide information on their financial performance, products and services, and other relevant factors.

Both primary and secondary research methods have their advantages and disadvantages. The choice of research method depends on the research objectives, available resources, and other relevant factors. By understanding the different types of market research available, businesses can select the most appropriate research method for their needs and gather the data necessary to make informed decisions.

In addition to the two main types of market research, primary and secondary research, there are also various sub-types of market research that businesses can use to gain a deeper understanding of their target market.

Here are a few examples:

Quantitative research:

This type of research involves collecting numerical data and analyzing it using statistical methods. Surveys, polls, and experiments are all examples of quantitative research methods. Quantitative research is useful for gathering large amounts of data quickly and identifying trends.

Qualitative research:

This type of research involves collecting non-numerical data and analyzing it to gain insights into people's attitudes, behaviors, and motivations. Interviews, focus groups, and observation are all examples of qualitative research methods. Qualitative research is useful for gaining a more in-depth understanding of people's experiences and preferences.

Exploratory research:

This type of research is used to explore new ideas or concepts and to gain a better understanding of a problem or opportunity. Exploratory research is often conducted before more focused research is carried out. Methods of exploratory research include literature reviews, pilot studies, and case studies.

Descriptive research:

This type of research is used to describe the characteristics of a population or phenomenon. Descriptive research often involves surveys or observational studies. The goal of descriptive research is to provide a detailed picture of a particular population or phenomenon.

Causal research:

This type of research is used to establish cause-and-effect relationships between variables. Experiments are the most common method of causal research. The goal of causal research is to determine whether one variable (the independent variable) has a causal effect on another variable (the dependent variable).

Understanding the different types of market research available can help businesses select the most appropriate research method for their needs and gather the data necessary to make informed decisions. By combining multiple research methods, businesses can gain a more comprehensive understanding of their target market and identify new opportunities for growth and innovation.

1.3 Common mistakes to avoid in market research

Here are some of the most common mistakes:

Not defining clear research objectives:

One of the most important steps in market research is defining clear research objectives. Without clear objectives, businesses may gather irrelevant or inaccurate data, wasting time and resources.

Using biased or leading questions:

The wording of survey questions can have a significant impact on the data that is collected. Using biased or leading questions can skew the results and lead to inaccurate conclusions.

Not considering the target audience:

It's important to consider the characteristics of the target audience when designing research methods. Failing to consider factors like age, gender, or socioeconomic status can lead to inaccurate or incomplete data.

Collecting insufficient or irrelevant data:

Collecting too little data can lead to incomplete insights, while collecting irrelevant data can waste resources. It's important to strike a balance and collect only the data that is necessary to achieve the research objectives.

Failing to account for bias or error:

All research methods are subject to bias and error, which can impact the accuracy of the data collected. It's important to identify and account for potential sources of bias or error to ensure that the data is as accurate as possible.

Ignoring the competition:

Market research should not only focus on the target market but also on the competition. Ignoring the competition can lead to missed opportunities and lost market share.

Not adapting to changing market conditions:

Market research should be an ongoing process that adapts to changing market conditions. Failing to adapt to new trends or changes in the market can lead to missed opportunities or even business failure.

By avoiding these common mistakes, businesses can ensure that their market research efforts are effective and lead to informed decision-making.

1.4 Defining the scope of market research

This involves identifying the specific questions that need to be answered, the target audience for the research, and the timeframe and budget for the research.

Defining the scope of market research is important because it helps to ensure that the research is focused and efficient. Here are some key considerations for defining the scope of market research:

Research objectives:

Before starting any market research, it's important to clearly define the objectives of the research. This involves identifying the specific questions that the research will answer, such as "What are the key factors that influence customer purchasing decisions in our industry?" or "What are the biggest challenges that our competitors are facing? »

Target audience:

It's important to identify the target audience for the research, which may include current customers, potential customers, or industry experts. Understanding the characteristics of the target audience, such as their age, gender, income level, and geographic location, can help to ensure that the research is focused and relevant.

Research methods:

There are many different research methods available, including surveys, interviews, focus groups, and observational studies. The scope of the research should take into account the strengths and weaknesses of each research method, as well as the resources and time available for the research.

Timeframe and budget:

Defining the scope of the research should also involve setting realistic timelines and budgets for the research. This may involve prioritizing research objectives based on their importance, as well as considering the resources available for the research.

By defining the scope of market research, businesses can ensure that their research efforts are focused, efficient, and effective in answering the specific questions that are most important to their success. This can help businesses to make informed decisions and gain a competitive edge in their industry.

Chapter 2: Developing a Market Research Plan

In this chapter, we will discuss the key steps involved in creating a market research plan that will help businesses to gather the information they need to make informed decisions and gain a competitive edge in their industry.

Effective market research requires careful planning and preparation. A well-designed market research plan can help businesses to define their research objectives, identify the target audience for the research, choose the most appropriate research methods, and ensure that the research is carried out within a realistic timeframe and budget.

In Chapter 2, we will discuss the following topics:

- Defining research objectives: The first step in developing a market research plan is to clearly define the objectives of the research. This involves identifying the specific questions that the research will answer and the outcomes that the business hopes to achieve.
- Identifying the target audience: The next step is to identify the target audience for the research. This may include current or potential customers, industry experts, or other stakeholders.
- Choosing research methods: Once the research objectives and target audience have been defined, the next step is to choose the most appropriate research methods. This may include surveys, interviews, focus groups, or observational studies.
- Creating a research timeline and budget: It's important to create a realistic timeline and budget for the research to ensure that it is carried out efficiently and effectively.
- Analyzing and reporting research findings: Once the research has been carried out, it's important to analyze the data and report the findings in a clear and concise manner.

By following these steps, businesses can develop a market research plan that will help them to gather the information they need to make informed decisions and gain a competitive edge in their industry.

2.1 Steps involved in developing a research plan

Here are the steps involved:

Define research objectives:

The first step in developing a market research plan is to define the research objectives. This involves identifying the specific questions that the research will answer and the outcomes that the business hopes to achieve. For example, the research objectives may include understanding customer needs and preferences, identifying market trends, or evaluating the effectiveness of marketing campaigns.

Identify the target audience:

The next step is to identify the target audience for the research. This may include current or potential customers, industry experts, or other stakeholders. Understanding the characteristics of the target audience, such as their age, gender, income level, and geographic location, can help to ensure that the research is focused and relevant.

Choose research methods:

Once the research objectives and target audience have been defined, the next step is to choose the most appropriate research methods. This may include surveys, interviews, focus groups, or observational studies. The choice of research methods will depend on factors such as the research objectives, the target audience, and the available resources.

Create a research timeline and budget:

It's important to create a realistic timeline and budget for the research to ensure that it is carried out efficiently and effectively. This may involve prioritizing research objectives based on their importance, as well as considering the resources available for the research.

Develop a data analysis and reporting plan:

Once the research has been carried out, it's important to analyze the data and report the findings in a clear and concise manner. This may involve using statistical analysis tools, developing charts and graphs to visualize the data, and preparing written reports or presentations to communicate the findings.

By following these steps, businesses can develop a market research plan that will help them to gather the information they need to make informed decisions and gain a competitive edge in their industry.

2.2 Understanding the research objectives

Here are some key points to consider when defining research objectives:

1. Identify the research questions:

The first step in defining research objectives is to identify the specific questions that the research will answer. For example, if the objective of the research is to understand customer needs and preferences, the research questions may include:

- What factors influence customers' purchasing decisions?
- What are customers' perceptions of our products or services?
- What do customers value most in a product or service?

2. Consider the business goals:

The research objectives should align with the broader goals of the business. For example, if the business goal is to increase market share, the research objectives may focus on understanding customer preferences for certain products or services, or identifying key areas of competitive advantage.

3. Determine the scope of the research:

Defining the scope of the research is important to ensure that the research objectives are achievable within the available resources and timeframe. This may involve prioritizing research questions based on their importance, or narrowing the focus of the research to a specific geographic region or customer segment.

4. Use SMART criteria:

To ensure that research objectives are specific, measurable, achievable, relevant, and time-bound, it can be helpful to use the SMART criteria. This involves setting objectives that are:

- Specific: Clearly defined and focused on a particular area of inquiry
- Measurable: Able to be quantified or measured in some way
- Achievable: Realistic and attainable within the available resources and timeframe
- Relevant: Aligned with the broader goals of the business and relevant to the target audience
- Time-bound: Defined within a specific timeframe

By carefully considering these factors when defining research objectives, businesses can develop a market research plan that is focused, achievable, and aligned with their broader goals.

2.3 Selecting the right research method

Here are some key considerations when selecting a research method:

Research objectives:

The research method should align with the research objectives. For example, if the objective of the research is to understand customer preferences, a survey or focus group may be appropriate, while if the objective is to observe customer behavior, an observational study may be more suitable.

Target audience:

The research method should also consider the target audience. For example, if the target audience is geographically dispersed, an online survey may be the most effective method, while if the target audience is a small group of industry experts, a one-on-one interview may be more appropriate.

Available resources:

The research method should also be feasible within the available resources, including time, budget, and staff. For example, conducting a large-scale survey may be time-consuming and costly, while conducting a small-scale observational study may be more feasible.

Data accuracy and reliability:

The research method should ensure that the data collected is accurate and reliable. For example, a survey with poorly designed questions or a small sample size may not provide accurate data, while an observational study with unclear criteria for data collection may not be reliable.

Ethical considerations:

The research method should also consider ethical considerations, such as ensuring informed consent and protecting the privacy of participants.

Some common research methods include surveys, interviews, focus groups, observational studies, and experiments. Each method has its own strengths and weaknesses, and the choice of method will depend on the specific research objectives and context.

By carefully considering these factors when selecting a research method, businesses can develop a market research plan that is effective in gathering relevant and accurate data to inform their decisions.

2.4 Determining the research budget

Developing a market research plan requires careful consideration of the costs involved in conducting the research.

Here are some key considerations when determining the research budget:

Research objectives:

The research budget should align with the research objectives. For example, if the objective of the research is to conduct a large-scale survey, the budget may need to include expenses related to survey software, data analysis tools, and participant incentives.

Research method:

The research method will also impact the budget. For example, conducting a one-on-one interview may be more expensive than conducting a focus group or survey.

Sample size:

The size of the sample will also impact the budget. A larger sample size may require a larger budget to cover participant incentives, data collection, and analysis.

Expertise:

If the business lacks the expertise to conduct the research internally, outsourcing to a research agency may be necessary, which may require a larger budget.

Timeframe:

The timeframe for the research will also impact the budget. Conducting research on a tight deadline may require additional resources or expedited services, which may come at a higher cost.

Contingency plan: It is important to have a contingency plan in place to account for unforeseen expenses or issues that may arise during the research process.

By carefully considering these factors when determining the research budget, businesses can develop a market research plan that is feasible within their available resources. It is important to remember that conducting thorough market research is an investment that can help businesses make informed decisions and ultimately save costs in the long run.

Chapter 3: Conducting Secondary Research

This chapter is important because secondary research is a cost-effective and efficient way to gather insights about the market and competition. In this chapter, we will explore the various sources of secondary research, including government publications, industry reports, academic journals, and online databases. We will also discuss how to evaluate the credibility and reliability of secondary sources, as well as how to effectively organize and analyze the information gathered through secondary research.

By the end of this chapter, readers will have a comprehensive understanding of how to conduct secondary research and how to use the insights gathered to inform business decisions.

3.1 Introduction to secondary research

Secondary research involves the collection and analysis of information from existing sources such as government publications, industry reports, academic journals, and online databases. This type of research is often less time-consuming and less expensive than primary research, which involves collecting information directly from the market or consumers.

Secondary research can provide valuable insights into the market, competition, and industry trends. It can help businesses identify potential opportunities, better understand their customers and competitors, and make informed decisions.

It is important to note that secondary research has some limitations. The information gathered may not be specific to the business or industry, and it may not be completely up-to-date or accurate. Therefore, it is important to evaluate the credibility and reliability of the sources used in secondary research.

In this section, we will discuss the advantages and disadvantages of secondary research, as well as how to effectively use secondary research to inform business decisions. We will also discuss how to evaluate the credibility and reliability of sources, and how to properly cite and document sources used in secondary research.

3.2 Sources of secondary research data

Here are some common sources of secondary research data:

Government publications:

Government agencies often collect and publish data related to demographics, economic trends, and industry statistics. These publications can be a valuable source of secondary research data for businesses.

Industry reports:

Industry reports are often produced by market research firms and provide comprehensive insights into specific industries. These reports can cover topics such as market size, trends, and competitive analysis.

Academic journals:

Academic journals are a valuable source of research articles written by scholars and researchers in a variety of fields. These articles can provide insights into consumer behavior, market trends, and industry developments.

Online databases:

There are a variety of online databases that provide access to secondary research data. For example, business databases like Factiva and ProQuest provide access to news articles, industry reports, and market research studies.

Company reports:

Company reports, such as annual reports and SEC filings, can provide valuable insights into a company's financial performance, market position, and strategic plans.

Trade associations:

Trade associations are organizations that represent specific industries or professions. These associations often provide data and research related to the industry they represent.

Social media:

Social media can be a valuable source of information for businesses, especially for insights into consumer behavior and sentiment.

By understanding the sources of secondary research data, businesses can effectively gather information to inform their decision-making processes. It is important to evaluate the credibility and reliability of the sources used in secondary research, and to properly cite and document the sources used.

3.3 Evaluating the quality of secondary research data

Here are some key factors to consider when evaluating the quality of secondary research data:

Relevance:

Is the data relevant to your research question or objective? Make sure that the data you are using is applicable to your specific research needs.

Credibility:

Is the source of the data reputable and trustworthy? Look for sources that are known for producing reliable and accurate information.

Objectivity:

Is the data presented objectively, or does it have a bias or agenda? It is important to use sources that present data objectively, without a specific agenda or bias.

Currency:

Is the data up-to-date and relevant to the current market or industry trends? Make sure that the data you are using is current and reflects the current state of the market or industry.

Methodology:

Was the data collected using a rigorous and reliable methodology? Look for sources that have used a valid and reliable research methodology.

Sample size and representativeness:

Was the data collected from a representative sample size? Make sure that the data you are using is based on a representative sample of the population or industry.

Limitations:

Are there any limitations to the data, such as sampling biases or methodological limitations? It is important to acknowledge any limitations to the data and take them into account when analyzing the data.

By evaluating the quality of secondary research data, businesses can ensure that they are making informed decisions based on reliable and accurate information. It is important to critically evaluate the sources of data and consider the context in which the data was collected.

3.4 Analyzing and interpreting secondary research data

Here are some key steps to follow when analyzing and interpreting secondary research data:

Organize the data:

Start by organizing the data into categories that are relevant to your research objective. This can help you to identify patterns and trends in the data.

Review the data:

Take a close look at the data to identify any outliers or anomalies that may impact your analysis.

Calculate key metrics:

Use statistical analysis to calculate key metrics such as averages, medians, and standard deviations. These metrics can help you to identify trends and patterns in the data.

Visualize the data:

Create charts, graphs, and other visualizations to help you better understand the data. Visualizations can help to highlight patterns and trends in the data that might not be immediately apparent from looking at the raw data.

Compare data sources:

If you are using multiple sources of secondary research data, compare the data to identify any discrepancies or inconsistencies. This can help you to identify any biases or limitations in the data.

Draw conclusions:

Based on your analysis of the data, draw conclusions that are relevant to your research objective. Make sure to support your conclusions with evidence from the data.

Communicate findings:

Present your findings in a clear and concise manner, using visualizations and other tools to help communicate your key findings. Make sure to provide context for your findings, including any limitations or biases in the data.

By following these steps, businesses can effectively analyze and interpret secondary research data to make informed decisions. It is important to be thorough and objective in your analysis, and to consider the context in which the data was collected.

Chapter 4: Designing a Research Questionnaire

A research questionnaire is a set of questions designed to gather information from respondents that can help businesses better understand their target market, customer needs, and preferences.

In this chapter, we will discuss the key steps involved in designing a research questionnaire, including defining research objectives, identifying the target audience, selecting the appropriate question format, and pre-testing the questionnaire. We will also explore the best practices for designing effective questions that are clear, concise, and unbiased.

By following the guidelines outlined in this chapter, businesses can design research questionnaires that provide valuable insights into their target market, helping them to make informed decisions and improve their products and services.

4.1 Understanding the purpose of a research questionnaire

The primary purpose of a research questionnaire is to gather information from respondents that can help businesses to better understand their target market, customer needs, and preferences. Questionnaires are a type of primary research method, which means that businesses collect data directly from their target audience, rather than relying on existing data sources like secondary research.

Research questionnaires can be used to collect a wide range of information, including demographic information, opinions, attitudes, and behaviors. They can be administered through a variety of channels, including online surveys, phone surveys, mail surveys, and in-person interviews.

The information gathered through research questionnaires can help businesses to make informed decisions about product development, marketing strategy, and customer service. For example, a business might use a research questionnaire to gather information about customer preferences for a new product or service. The data collected through the questionnaire can help the business to make decisions about product design, pricing, and marketing messaging.

Research questionnaires are an essential tool for businesses looking to gain deeper insights into their target market. By understanding the purpose of a research questionnaire, businesses can design effective questionnaires that provide valuable insights and help them to make informed decisions.

4.2 Components of a research questionnaire

There are several components that are essential to include in a research questionnaire to ensure that it is effective in collecting the necessary data. These components include:

Introduction:

The introduction of the questionnaire should provide a brief overview of the purpose of the survey, explain why the respondent's participation is important, and provide any necessary instructions or guidelines for completing the survey.

Demographic questions:

Demographic questions are used to gather basic information about the respondent, such as age, gender, education level, income, and occupation. This information can be used to segment the data and analyze the results by different demographic groups.

Research questions:

The research questions are the heart of the questionnaire and should be designed to gather specific information about the research topic. They should be clear, concise, and unbiased to ensure that the data collected is accurate and reliable.

Question format:

The question format refers to the way in which the questions are presented to the respondent. Question formats can include multiple-choice questions, open-ended questions, rating scales, and more. The question format should be selected based on the type of information being collected and the target audience.

Response options:

Response options are the choices that are provided to the respondent when answering a question. They should be designed to be clear and concise, and provide accurate and relevant information that is aligned with the research objectives.

Conclusion:

The conclusion of the questionnaire should thank the respondent for their participation and provide any necessary information about the follow-up process, such as how the results will be used and when they will be available.

By including these components in a research questionnaire, businesses can design effective questionnaires that provide valuable insights into their target m

4.3 Types of research questions

There are two main types of research questions: closed-ended questions and open-ended questions.

Closed-ended questions:

Closed-ended questions are questions that offer respondents a limited number of response options, such as yes/no questions, multiple choice questions, or Likert scale questions. These questions are useful when researchers want to measure specific attitudes or opinions or when they need to quantify data. The advantage of closed-ended questions is that they are easy to analyze, and results can be easily compared across respondents.

Open-ended questions:

Open-ended questions are questions that allow respondents to provide more detailed and personalized responses. These questions typically begin with "why," "how," or "what," and require more thought and effort on the part of the respondent. Open-ended questions are useful when researchers want to gather detailed information or explore a particular issue in-depth. The advantage of open-ended questions is that they provide rich and detailed data, but analyzing the data can be time-consuming and difficult.

Within these two main categories, there are several different types of research questions that can be used in a questionnaire, including:

- Dichotomous questions: These are questions with only two possible answers, such as yes/no questions.

- Multiple-choice questions: These questions offer respondents a selection of options from which to choose.

- Ranking questions: These questions ask respondents to rank items in order of preference or importance.

- Likert scale questions: These questions ask respondents to rate their level of agreement or disagreement with a statement on a scale, typically ranging from "strongly agree" to "strongly disagree. »

- Semantic differential questions: These questions ask respondents to rate a concept or object on a scale between two opposite adjectives, such as "happy-sad" or « hot-cold."

By understanding the different types of research questions that can be used in a questionnaire, researchers can select the appropriate questions to gather the necessary data and ensure that their research objectives are met.

4.4 Pre-testing a research questionnaire

Pre-testing is the process of testing a questionnaire with a small group of individuals who are similar to the target population to identify any issues or errors that need to be addressed before administering the questionnaire to the larger population.

There are several reasons why pre-testing a questionnaire is important:

Identify unclear or confusing questions:

Pre-testing can help identify questions that are unclear or confusing to respondents. This can be done through asking respondents for feedback on the questions or by observing their behavior when answering the questions.

Determine the appropriate length of the questionnaire:

Pre-testing can help determine the appropriate length of the questionnaire, which can impact response rates and data quality. If the questionnaire is too long, respondents may become fatigued or lose interest, leading to incomplete or inaccurate responses.

Test the flow and sequence of questions:

Pre-testing can help ensure that the flow and sequence of questions is logical and easy to follow for respondents.

Test the reliability and validity of the questionnaire:

Pre-testing can help identify potential issues with the reliability and validity of the questionnaire, which can impact the accuracy and usefulness of the data collected.

To pre-test a research questionnaire, researchers typically recruit a small sample of individuals who are similar to the target population and administer the questionnaire to them. Researchers can then collect feedback from the respondents on their experience with the questionnaire, including any issues they encountered or questions they found unclear. Based on this feedback, researchers can revise and improve the questionnaire before administering it to the larger population.

By pre-testing a research questionnaire, researchers can ensure that the questionnaire is clear, concise, and effective in collecting the necessary data to meet their research objectives.

Chapter 5: Conducting Primary Research

Primary research is often necessary when secondary research is insufficient or when more specific information is needed to answer research questions.

This chapter will cover the various methods of primary research, including surveys, interviews, focus groups, and observational studies. It will also cover the key steps involved in conducting primary research, such as selecting the target population, designing the research instrument, collecting the data, and analyzing the results.

Conducting primary research can be time-consuming and resource-intensive, but it can also provide valuable insights and data that are specific to the research objectives. By following the guidelines and best practices outlined in this chapter, researchers can ensure that their primary research is effective and efficient in collecting the necessary data to meet their research objectives.

5.1 Introduction to primary research

Primary research involves collecting new data directly from the target population, as opposed to secondary research which involves analyzing existing data sources. Primary research methods can include surveys, interviews, focus groups, and observational studies.

Primary research is often necessary when more specific information is required to answer research questions or when existing data sources are insufficient or outdated. It can provide unique insights and data that are specific to the research objectives, and can help to validate or challenge assumptions that were made during the secondary research phase.

However, primary research can be time-consuming and expensive, especially if a large sample size is required. It also requires careful planning and execution to ensure that the data collected is reliable and valid.

It is important to determine the appropriate primary research method based on the research objectives, target population, and available resources. This chapter will provide guidance on the steps involved in conducting primary research, including selecting the appropriate method, designing the research instrument, collecting the data, and analyzing the results.

5.2 Types of primary research

There are several types of primary research methods that can be used to gather new data directly from the target population. Some of the most common primary research methods include:

1. Surveys:

Surveys involve asking a series of questions to a sample of individuals or groups to gather data about their attitudes, behaviors, and opinions. Surveys can be conducted through various channels, such as online surveys, phone surveys, or in-person surveys.

2. Interviews:

Interviews involve one-on-one conversations between the researcher and the respondent to gather more in-depth and detailed information about their experiences, attitudes, or behaviors. Interviews can be conducted in person, over the phone, or via video conferencing.

3. Focus groups:

Focus groups involve a small group of individuals who are brought together to discuss a specific topic or product. The researcher facilitates the discussion and encourages participants to share their thoughts, opinions, and experiences. Focus groups can provide rich and detailed data, but are often more time-consuming and expensive than other methods.

4. Observational studies:

Observational studies involve observing and recording the behaviors of individuals or groups in a natural setting. This method is often used in marketing research to understand how consumers interact with products or services in real-life situations.

The choice of primary research method will depend on the research objectives, the target population, and the available resources. Each method has its own advantages and limitations, and researchers should carefully consider which method is most appropriate for their specific research needs.

5.3 Sampling methods

Sampling is an important aspect of primary research, as it involves selecting a representative subset of the target population to gather data from.

Here are some common sampling methods used in primary research:

Probability sampling:

This type of sampling involves selecting a random sample from the target population, where each individual or group in the population has an equal chance of being selected. Probability sampling methods include simple random sampling, stratified sampling, and cluster sampling.

Non-probability sampling:

This type of sampling does not involve random selection, and therefore does not guarantee that the sample is representative of the target population. Non-probability sampling methods include convenience sampling, purposive sampling, and snowball sampling.

Quota sampling:

Quota sampling involves selecting a sample that reflects the characteristics of the target population, such as age, gender, or income. This method is often used in market research to ensure that the sample is representative of the population in terms of key demographic variables.

Multi-stage sampling:

Multi-stage sampling involves selecting a sample in multiple stages, where the sample is gradually narrowed down from a larger group to a smaller group. This method is often used in large-scale studies where it is not feasible to select a random sample from the entire target population.

Choosing the right sampling method is crucial to ensure that the sample is representative of the target population and that the data gathered is reliable and valid. The choice of sampling method will depend on the research objectives, the characteristics of the target population, and the available resources.

5.4 Data collection methods

There are several data collection methods that can be used in primary research, and the choice of method will depend on the research objectives, the target population, and the available resources.

Here are some common data collection methods used in primary research:

Surveys:

Surveys involve asking a set of standardized questions to a sample of the target population. Surveys can be conducted in person, by phone, or online.

Interviews:

Interviews involve asking open-ended or structured questions to individuals or groups in the target population. Interviews can be conducted in person, by phone, or online.

Focus groups:

Focus groups involve bringing together a small group of individuals from the target population to discuss a specific topic or issue in-depth. Focus groups are often used in market research to gather qualitative data on consumer preferences and opinions.

Observations:

Observations involve observing and recording the behavior of individuals or groups in the target population. Observations can be conducted in natural settings, such as a retail store or a public space, or in a controlled laboratory setting.

Experiments:

Experiments involve manipulating one or more variables to determine their effect on a specific outcome. Experiments are often used in scientific research to test hypotheses and establish cause-and-effect relationships.

Choosing the right data collection method is crucial to ensure that the data gathered is reliable and valid, and that the research objectives are met. The choice of data collection method will depend on the research questions, the target population, and the available resources.

Chapter 6: Data Analysis

Chapter 6 focuses on data analysis, which is a crucial part of the market research process. After collecting data through primary or secondary research methods, the next step is to analyze the data to draw meaningful conclusions and insights.

Data analysis involves organizing, cleaning, and interpreting the data to identify patterns, trends, and relationships that can inform business decisions. This chapter will cover various data analysis techniques, including statistical analysis, qualitative analysis, and data visualization. It will also discuss software tools that can be used for data analysis, such as Excel, SPSS, and Tableau.

Effective data analysis can provide valuable insights into consumer behavior, market trends, and business performance. By understanding the data, businesses can make informed decisions, develop effective marketing strategies, and improve their overall competitiveness in the market.

In this chapter, we will explore various techniques and tools for data analysis, as well as best practices for ensuring the accuracy and validity of the findings.

6.1 Introduction to data analysis

Data analysis is the process of cleaning, organizing, interpreting, and drawing conclusions from raw data. It is a critical step in the market research process because it allows businesses to make informed decisions based on evidence rather than assumptions or intuition.

Data analysis can involve both quantitative and qualitative methods. Quantitative analysis involves using statistical methods to analyze numerical data, such as sales figures, customer demographics, or website traffic. Qualitative analysis involves analyzing non-numerical data, such as customer feedback, interviews, or open-ended survey responses.

The main goal of data analysis is to identify patterns, trends, and relationships in the data that can help businesses gain insights into consumer behavior, market trends, and business performance. By understanding the data, businesses can make informed decisions, develop effective marketing strategies, and improve their overall competitiveness in the market.

6.2 Types of data analysis techniques

There are several types of data analysis techniques that can be used in market research. Here are a few examples:

Descriptive analysis:

This technique is used to describe the basic features of the data in a study, such as the frequency of responses, mean, median, and mode. It provides a summary of the data that can help identify patterns and trends.

Inferential analysis:

This technique is used to make inferences about the population based on the sample data. It involves using statistical tests, such as hypothesis testing, to determine the probability that the findings are representative of the population.

Regression analysis:

This technique is used to analyze the relationship between two or more variables. It helps to identify the strength and direction of the relationship and can be used to make predictions about future outcomes.

Factor analysis:

This technique is used to identify underlying factors or dimensions that explain the variation in a set of variables. It helps to simplify complex data by grouping variables that are related to each other.

Cluster analysis:

This technique is used to group objects or individuals that have similar characteristics. It helps to identify subgroups within the data and can be useful in segmentation analysis.

Text analysis:

This technique is used to analyze textual data, such as customer feedback or social media posts. It helps to identify common themes and sentiments in the data and can be used to gain insights into customer attitudes and opinions.

Each technique has its strengths and weaknesses, and the choice of technique will depend on the research questions and data being analyzed.

6.3 Preparing data for analysis

Before data can be analyzed, it must be prepared appropriately. This involves several steps, including data cleaning, coding, and entry. Data cleaning involves checking the data for errors or missing values and correcting them. For example, if a respondent did not answer a question, the researcher may need to determine whether the response was intentional or accidental.

After the data has been cleaned, it needs to be coded. This involves assigning a numeric value or category to each response, which makes it easier to analyze the data. For example, if respondents were asked about their age, their responses may be coded as "18-24", "25-34", "35-44", and so on.

Once the data has been cleaned and coded, it is ready to be entered into a computer program for analysis. This is typically done using a spreadsheet or statistical software, such as SPSS or SAS.

It is important to note that the quality of the data analysis depends heavily on the quality of the data preparation. Poorly prepared data can lead to inaccurate or unreliable results. Therefore, it is crucial to take the time to ensure that the data is properly cleaned, coded, and entered before beginning the analysis.

6.4 Analyzing and interpreting research findings

To begin with, data analysis requires the researcher to examine the data collected to determine if it is consistent with their research objectives. The researcher then needs to clean the data, which involves checking for errors, missing data, or anomalies, before starting the analysis.

After cleaning the data, the researcher can then begin to analyze the data. The analysis can be done using both qualitative and quantitative techniques, depending on the type of data and research questions. Common quantitative techniques used include descriptive statistics, regression analysis, and correlation analysis. Qualitative techniques, on the other hand, include content analysis, thematic analysis, and discourse analysis.

Once the analysis is complete, the researcher can begin to interpret the results. Interpreting the results involves examining the findings and drawing meaningful conclusions from them. It is essential to ensure that the conclusions are consistent with the research objectives and that the results are communicated clearly and effectively to stakeholders.

Data analysis is a crucial part of market research that involves cleaning, analyzing, and interpreting data collected during primary and secondary research. The techniques used for analysis depend on the type of data and research questions. Interpreting the findings is essential to draw meaningful conclusions that are consistent with the research objectives.

Chapter 7: Reporting and Presenting Research Findings

Chapter 7 focuses on the critical step of reporting and presenting the research findings. It's not enough to simply conduct research and analyze data; you must also effectively communicate the results to stakeholders in a clear and concise manner. This chapter will cover the essential components of a research report, best practices for presenting data visually, and tips for effectively communicating your findings to different audiences. By the end of this chapter, you will have a comprehensive understanding of how to create a compelling and impactful research report that effectively communicates your research findings to key stakeholders.

7.1 The purpose of research reporting

the purpose of research reporting is to communicate the findings of the market research study in a clear, concise, and effective manner to the stakeholders. The research report serves as a crucial tool for decision-making and enables stakeholders to make informed decisions based on the data and insights gathered from the research.

A well-written research report should include the objectives of the study, the research methodology used, the findings and insights obtained from the research, and the conclusions and recommendations based on the findings. The report should be structured in a logical and organized way, with clear headings and subheadings to help the reader navigate the content.

The research report should be written in a style that is appropriate for the target audience. For example, if the report is intended for a technical audience, the language and terminology used should be more technical, whereas if the report is intended for a non-technical audience, the language and terminology used should be simplified and more accessible.

The purpose of research reporting is to present the findings and insights of the market research study in a way that is meaningful, relevant, and actionable for the stakeholders.

7.2 Writing a research report

Writing a research report is an essential part of the research process. A well-written research report serves as a valuable tool for communicating research findings to key stakeholders. Here are some key components of a research report:

Introduction:

The introduction sets the stage for the research report and includes a brief summary of the research problem, objectives, and methodology.

Literature Review:

The literature review summarizes existing research on the topic and provides a context for the study.

Methodology:

This section provides a detailed description of the research design, sampling technique, data collection method, and data analysis approach.

Results:

The results section presents the findings of the study, including statistical data and other relevant information.

Discussion:

The discussion section interprets the findings of the study and provides insights into their significance.

Conclusion:

The conclusion summarizes the study's main findings and their implications for the research problem.

Recommendations:

This section offers practical suggestions for addressing the research problem and implementing changes based on the study's findings.

In writing a research report, it's important to keep in mind the intended audience and to use clear, concise language. The report should be well-organized, and the information should be presented in a logical manner.

Graphs, tables, and other visual aids can be used to enhance the report and make the data more accessible to readers. Finally, the report should be carefully proofread to ensure that it is free from errors and meets professional standards.

7.3 Creating effective visual aids

When presenting research findings, creating effective visual aids can be an impactful way to communicate your results to your audience. Visual aids such as charts, graphs, tables, and diagrams can make complex data more easily digestible and can help highlight key findings.

To create effective visual aids, it's important to consider the type of data you are presenting and choose the appropriate visual representation. For example, if you are presenting numerical data, a bar chart or line graph may be appropriate, while if you are presenting categorical data, a pie chart or histogram may be more suitable.

It's also important to make sure that the visual aid is easy to read and understand. This means using clear labels, avoiding clutter, and using appropriate colors and formatting.

In addition to visual aids, it can also be helpful to provide a written explanation of your findings to help your audience understand the context and significance of your results. This can include a summary of key findings, an explanation of any limitations or caveats, and recommendations for future research or action.

Creating effective visual aids and presenting research findings in a clear and concise manner can help ensure that your audience understands the significance of your research and its implications.

7.4 Presenting research findings

Presenting research findings is an important part of the market research process. Once the data has been collected, analyzed, and interpreted, it needs to be communicated to the relevant stakeholders. The presentation of research findings should be designed to effectively convey the results to the intended audience.

There are several factors to consider when presenting research findings. One key consideration is the format of the presentation. Different audiences may respond better to different formats, such as a written report, a PowerPoint presentation, or an in-person presentation. The format chosen should be tailored to the needs of the audience and the purpose of the research.

Another important factor to consider is the visual aids used in the presentation. Effective visual aids can help to clarify complex information and make it easier for the audience to understand. Examples of effective visual aids include graphs, charts, tables, and diagrams. The visual aids used should be carefully selected to support the key findings and enhance the overall presentation.

In addition to the format and visual aids, it is also important to consider the tone and language used in the presentation. The presentation should be clear, concise, and easy to understand. Technical jargon should be avoided or explained clearly, especially if the audience is not familiar with the subject matter.

The presentation of research findings should be designed to effectively communicate the results of the research to the intended audience in a clear, concise, and visually appealing manner.

Chapter 8: Applying Market Research Findings

After conducting extensive research and analyzing data, it is essential to apply the findings to the business. In this chapter, we will discuss the ways in which entrepreneurs can use the information obtained from market research to improve their business operations, make informed decisions, and develop effective marketing strategies.

The chapter will provide insights into the practical applications of market research findings in various business aspects, including product development, pricing, promotion, and distribution. The importance of aligning research results with business goals and objectives will be emphasized, and the strategies for implementing research findings effectively will be explored.

Entrepreneurs need to apply the insights gained from market research to stay competitive and meet the changing needs of their customers. Therefore, this chapter will provide valuable guidance on the process of using market research findings to develop a competitive advantage, make data-driven decisions, and achieve business success.

8.1 The role of market research in decision-making

By conducting market research, businesses can make informed decisions about product development, pricing, promotion, and distribution strategies.
Without market research, businesses may make assumptions about their target market and the demand for their products or services, which can result in costly mistakes. For example, launching a product without conducting market research can lead to a failure to meet customer needs, a lack of demand, and ultimately, loss of revenue.

Understanding the role of market research in decision-making is essential for any business that wants to succeed in today's competitive market. In this chapter, we will explore how to apply market research findings to make strategic decisions that will help businesses achieve their goals.

8.2 Identifying opportunities and threats

After conducting market research, businesses can identify both opportunities and threats in their target market. By analyzing data and understanding consumer behavior, businesses can identify gaps in the market or areas where they can improve their products or services. This can help businesses create a competitive advantage and increase their market share. Additionally, market research can also identify potential threats, such as new competitors, changing consumer preferences, or shifts in the market.

For example, if a business is in the restaurant industry and conducts market research, they may find that there is a high demand for plant-based menu options. This could present an opportunity for the business to create a new line of plant-based dishes and attract a new segment of customers. On the other hand, the market research may reveal that a new competitor is entering the market with a similar concept. This could be a potential threat to the business and they may need to reposition themselves or differentiate their offerings to remain competitive.

In short, market research helps businesses identify opportunities to grow and expand, as well as potential threats to their success.

8.3 Developing marketing strategies

Developing marketing strategies is a crucial aspect of applying market research findings. Once the research data has been analyzed and interpreted, businesses can use the insights gained from the research to inform their marketing strategies.

For example, market research can help businesses identify their target market and understand their preferences, behaviors, and needs. This information can be used to create targeted marketing campaigns that resonate with the target audience and increase the likelihood of conversions.

Market research can also help businesses identify gaps in the market or areas where they can differentiate themselves from competitors. This information can be used to develop unique value propositions and create marketing messaging that stands out in the marketplace.

Market research can inform decisions related to product development and pricing strategies. By understanding consumer preferences and behaviors, businesses can develop products that meet their needs and price them appropriately to increase sales and profitability.

The insights gained from market research are essential for developing effective marketing strategies that drive business growth and success.

8.4 Monitoring and evaluating marketing performance

Monitoring and evaluating marketing performance is a crucial step in the market research process. Once you have implemented your marketing strategies, it is important to track and measure their effectiveness to determine if they are achieving the desired results. This involves analyzing sales data, customer feedback, and other relevant metrics to evaluate the success of your marketing efforts.

One common approach to monitoring and evaluating marketing performance is to use Key Performance Indicators (KPIs), which are specific metrics that are used to measure progress towards achieving marketing objectives. KPIs can include metrics such as sales revenue, customer retention rates, website traffic, social media engagement, and more. By regularly tracking these metrics, you can identify areas of strength and weakness in your marketing campaigns, and make adjustments as needed to improve overall performance.

Another important aspect of monitoring and evaluating marketing performance is conducting ongoing customer research. This can involve collecting feedback through surveys, focus groups, or other methods to gain insights into customer preferences, behaviors, and attitudes. By gathering this information, you can better understand your target audience and develop marketing strategies that are tailored to their needs and interests.

Monitoring and evaluating marketing performance is a critical part of the market research process. By regularly tracking and measuring the effectiveness of your marketing efforts, you can identify opportunities for improvement and make informed decisions about future marketing investments.

Chapter 9: Emerging Trends in Market Research

In the constantly evolving landscape of business and technology, market research has become more important than ever before. With the advent of new technologies and changing consumer behaviors, businesses need to stay up-to-date with the latest trends and insights to stay ahead of the competition. Chapter 9 explores some of the emerging trends in market research and how they are changing the way businesses approach data collection and analysis. From the increasing use of artificial intelligence and machine learning, to the growing importance of social media and mobile research, this chapter highlights some of the newest and most exciting developments in the field of market research. By staying abreast of these trends, businesses can gain a deeper understanding of their customers and the market, leading to better decision-making and ultimately, increased success.

9.1 Introduction to emerging trends

The world of market research is constantly evolving, with new technologies and methodologies emerging all the time. As businesses strive to stay ahead of the competition and understand their customers better, market research professionals must stay up-to-date with the latest trends and techniques.

In this chapter, we will explore some of the emerging trends in market research, including the increasing use of artificial intelligence and machine learning, the rise of mobile research, the growing importance of data privacy and security, and the shift towards more agile research methods. We will also discuss the challenges and opportunities presented by these trends, and how market research professionals can adapt to these changes to stay competitive in a rapidly changing industry.

9.2 Artificial intelligence and machine learning in market research

Artificial intelligence (AI) and machine learning (ML) are two emerging trends that are transforming the field of market research. AI refers to the ability of computer systems to perform tasks that typically require human intelligence, such as recognizing speech, understanding natural language, and making decisions. ML, on the other hand, is a subset of AI that focuses on developing algorithms that can learn from and make predictions on data.

The use of AI and ML in market research allows for more efficient and accurate data collection, analysis, and interpretation. For example, AI-powered chatbots and voice assistants can be used to collect data from survey respondents in a conversational manner, while ML algorithms can be used to automatically categorize and analyze large amounts of unstructured data, such as social media posts and customer reviews.

Another way AI and ML are being used in market research is through predictive modeling. By analyzing historical data and identifying patterns and trends, these models can make predictions about future consumer behavior and help companies make more informed decisions about their marketing strategies.

It is important to note that the use of AI and ML in market research also raises ethical concerns, such as privacy and bias issues. As such, it is important for market researchers to carefully consider these issues and take steps to ensure that their use of AI and ML is both effective and ethical.

9.3 Big data and predictive analytics

In recent years, the amount of data generated by consumers and businesses has grown exponentially, giving rise to the field of big data. Big data refers to the large volume, velocity, and variety of data that are generated by people, devices, and machines, and can be difficult to process and analyze using traditional methods.

To address this challenge, market researchers are increasingly turning to predictive analytics, a technique that uses statistical algorithms and machine learning to analyze large data sets and identify patterns, trends, and insights that can inform business decisions.

By leveraging big data and predictive analytics, market researchers can gain a more nuanced understanding of consumer behavior and preferences, identify new market opportunities, and develop more effective marketing strategies. For example, predictive analytics can be used to identify which customers are most likely to purchase a particular product, enabling marketers to target their advertising and promotions more effectively.

Big data and predictive analytics are transforming the field of market research, allowing researchers to gain deeper insights into consumer behavior and preferences than ever before.

9.4 Ethical considerations in market research.

As with any field, ethical considerations are important in market research to ensure that research is conducted in a fair and responsible manner. Here are some key points to consider:

Informed consent:

It's important that research participants understand what they are consenting to, and that they are not coerced or misled in any way. Participants should be given clear information about the purpose of the research, how their data will be used, and any risks or benefits involved.

Privacy and confidentiality:

Researchers must take steps to protect participants' privacy and ensure that their data is kept confidential. This might involve anonymizing data, using secure storage and transfer methods, and limiting access to the data to only those who need it.

Avoiding harm:

Researchers should ensure that their research does not cause harm to participants or to the broader community. This might involve taking steps to minimize any risks associated with the research, and ensuring that any potential benefits are not outweighed by the risks.

Fairness and respect:

Research should be conducted in a fair and respectful manner, without bias or discrimination. This means avoiding any language or behavior that might be offensive or disrespectful, and ensuring that all participants are treated equally and with respect.

Compliance with regulations:

Researchers must ensure that they comply with all relevant regulations and guidelines, both in terms of the research itself and the way that data is collected, stored, and used.

Ethical considerations are an essential part of market research, and should be taken seriously by all researchers. By following best practices and being mindful of potential ethical issues, researchers can help to ensure that their research is conducted in a responsible and respectful manner.

Conclusion

In conclusion, market research is a crucial aspect of any successful business strategy. It allows businesses to gather insights about their target market, competitors, and industry trends, and use this information to make informed decisions. Developing a market research plan involves several important steps, including understanding research objectives, selecting the right research method, and determining the research budget.

Secondary research is an essential component of the market research process, as it provides valuable information about the market and industry. Understanding sources of secondary research data and how to evaluate their quality is important for ensuring that the information gathered is accurate and reliable. Once secondary research data has been collected, it can be analyzed and interpreted to gain insights about the market.

Designing a research questionnaire is another critical step in the market research process. The purpose of a research questionnaire is to collect data directly from respondents. Creating effective research questionnaires involves understanding the purpose of the questionnaire, selecting the appropriate components, and using the right types of research questions. Pre testing the questionnaire before administering it to respondents can help ensure that the questionnaire is effective.

Primary research involves collecting data directly from respondents through methods such as surveys, interviews, and focus groups. Sampling methods are essential in primary research, as they help ensure that the data collected is representative of the target population. Data collection methods such as online surveys and mobile surveys are becoming increasingly popular in the market research industry.

Once data has been collected, it must be analyzed and interpreted. There are several types of data analysis techniques available, including descriptive statistics, inferential statistics, and data visualization. Preparing data for analysis involves cleaning and organizing it to make it suitable for analysis.

Reporting and presenting research findings is the final step in the market research process. Writing a research report involves summarizing the research objectives, methods, findings, and conclusions. Creating effective visual aids such as charts and graphs can help make the findings more engaging and understandable for stakeholders. Presenting research findings to stakeholders is an opportunity to communicate the results and recommend actions based on the findings.

Emerging trends in market research include the use of artificial intelligence and machine learning, big data and predictive analytics, and ethical considerations. AI and machine learning can help automate certain aspects of the market research process and make it more efficient. Big data and predictive analytics can help businesses gain insights about their customers and predict their behavior. Ethical considerations are becoming increasingly important in market research, as businesses are held to higher standards of accountability for the data they collect and how they use it.

In conclusion, market research is essential for businesses to make informed decisions and develop effective strategies. Developing a comprehensive market research plan, conducting secondary and primary research, analyzing and interpreting data, and presenting research findings are all important steps in the market research process. As emerging technologies continue to impact the market research industry, businesses must stay up-to-date with these trends and incorporate them into their strategies to stay competitive.